TREETURE CREATURES

AND

FLOWERBUDS

Published in the United Kingdom by:

Blue Falcon Publishing
The Mill, Pury Hill Business Park,
Alderton Road, Towcester
Northamptonshire
NN12 7LS
Email: books@bluefalconpublishing.co.uk
Web: www.bluefalconpublishing.co.uk

A CIP record of this book is available from the British Library.

First printed July 2021

ISBN 9781912765416

Use your pocket guide,
when you go outside.
The leaves are at the back.
Take some snaps of who you track.
Share with us the ones you find,
To our buds and trees, be kind.

Oaky

Belongs to...

The Oak Tree

The king of the trees and can live up to 1000 years old.

They produce acorns in little woody cups.

Wood from an oak made the ships for the battle of Trafalgar.

The oak leaf was featured on an old sixpence coin.

Alder

Belongs to...

The Alder Tree

—

Magical myth: The Alder flowers dye the clothes of the fairies dark green so they can hide amongst the leaves.

They produce clusters of small cones.

The alder likes wet ground.

The leaves are like little hearts.

Rowan

Belongs to...

The Rowan Tree
—

Folklore belief: The rowan is a magical protector and keeps witches at bay.

They produce red berries in autumn after a white flower blossom.

They grow on higher ground.

The old Celtic name is wizards' tree.

Holly

Belongs to...

The Holly Tree
—

Myth: Thought to be bad luck to cut a holly tree down.

They produce red berries.

Holly wood is the whitest of all wood.

The branches and berries are used to decorate at Christmas time.

Willow

Belongs to...

The Willow Tree

In biblical times willow trees were celebratory.

The white willow is the largest of the willow trees and usually near water.

They produce catkins in early spring.

The willow tree wood is used for making cricket bats.

Field Maple

Belongs to...

The Field Maple Tree

Myth: Put a maple branch at your door and it is said no bats will enter.

They produce winged fruits.

In autumn they go a beautiful golden yellow.

The wood is used to make cellos.

Maple syrup comes from the sap of the field maple.

Hazel

Belongs to...

The Hazel Tree
—

Myth: The hazel tree has a magical power.

They have yellow catkins that look like lambs' tails.

They produce hazelnuts and the flowers feed nectar to bees.

Hazel wood is used for water divining.

Ash

Belongs to...

The Ash Tree

Myth: Thought to have medicinal and mystical character. The wood was burnt to scare evil spirits

They produce winged fruits – known as keys in the summer and autumn.

They have black velvety buds in the winter.

They can live up to 400 years old.

Beech

Belongs to...

The Beech Tree

—

Considered the queen of British trees and they can live for hundreds of years.

They produce beech masts as prickly seed cases.

The oil from the beech was used to burn lamps.

Sycamore

Belongs to...

The Sycamore Tree

—

They can grow up to 35 meters and live for up to 400 years.

The v-shaped winged fruits spin like helicopters when they fall.

Breadboards and other kitchen utensils are made from sycamore wood.

They are part of the maple family.

Spruce

Belongs to...

The Spruce Tree

Considered the tree for festive occasions.
Prince Albert decorated his spruce with candles
which started the Christmas tree tradition.

The spruce originates from Norway. They are
evergreen and have short needles.

They produce long cones that feed squirrels.

They can grow up to 40 meters tall, to a pointed
crown and live up to 1,000 years.

Horse Chestnut

Belongs to...

The Horse Chestnut Tree

—

hey can live up to 300 years and grow up to 40 meters high.

They produce the horse chestnut seed which is known as the conker, in spiky green cases.

It is said that the conkers keep spiders away.

Choose a 'champion' conker and battle with an opponent to see which one splits first.

The
TREE
TRAIL

Did you see me?

 Oaky

 Willow

 Beech

 Alder

 Field Maple

 Sycamore

 Rowan

 Horse Chestnut

 Spruce

 Holly

Ash

 Hazel

Trees take in Carbon Dioxide (CO2) and change it into Oxygen (O2) for us to breathe. This process is called photosynthesis. As a result of this trees are vital. Therefore, the more we have, the more we can slow the effects of global warming. With enough light, the tree absorbs the CO2 and water, changing it into glucose and oxygen. This ensures our atmosphere stays oxygen rich. Our wonderful trees can also improve the air quality by catching airborne particles of pollution which, can reduce smog levels.

Treeture Creatures and Flowerbuds
Book 1 – Oaky the Oak Leaf

In this story, we follow Oaky the oak leaf on his exciting adventure as he tries to make his way back home and meets some unfamiliar characters on the way!

Available to buy from Amazon, Waterstones and Foyles.

Treeture Creatures and Flowerbuds
Book 2 – Willow the Willow Leaf

It's Willow's turn for an adventure this time, as the little leaf finds himself washed downstream and makes many new friends as he tries to find his way back to where he belongs.

Available to buy from Amazon, Waterstones and Foyles.

Treeture Creatures and Flowerbuds
Book 3 – Beech the Beech Leaf

TREETURE CREATURES AND FLOWERBUDS

Beech the **Beech Leaf**

illustrated by
Gaynor Volpi

Marian Hawkins

When an unsuspecting beech leaf is whisked away on a ball, she learns a lot about the trees and flowers that surround her as she bounces, floats and squelches her way back to her beloved beech tree!

Available to buy from Amazon, Waterstones and Foyles.

Notes

Lightning Source UK Ltd.
Milton Keynes UK
UKHW021653110921
390183UK00010B/122